Praise f

Naomi Lowinsky's *Death and His Lorca* is a powerful volume of poems about love, about loss but also about how lost ones still stream indelibly through a life. Though the book touches on Jungian symbols of The Self, The Anima and Animus, mostly it presents The Shadow: the fire, the wild and unknown as poems probe the lives and legacy of grandparents, parents, lovers, spouses. Again and again, Lorca's passion and Lowinsky's intertwine, adding a memorable musical lyric to the whole book. In a literal yet metaphoric way the forever question being asked by this poet is: "Who has the passports?/Must she cross/the border alone?"

   – Susan Terris, author of *Familiar Tense*

The poems in *Death and His Lorca*, by Naomi Ruth Lowinsky, contain many deaths and close encounters with mortality, but the book is as much about life as about death. Lowinsky tells the stories of the lost and channels Barack Obama's grandmother, Madelyn Dunham, as movingly as she channels her own. And there is much dancing – dances for the dead and of the dead. In "Flamenco Dancer," which opens the collection, the dancer's "spine / is a wild and supple snake" as she arouses the spirits; in "The Russian Woman's Daughter," the "dead do a circle / dance around us." Lowinsky is equally at home with the facts of history, "the grim trains   the grieving / skies of northern / Europe," and the realm of myth and dream, where a daughter of Atatürk can show her a library of books "on the unearthed goddess." Beauty and mystery are abundant in this collection. Despite death's tenacity, it's an inspiring read.

   – Lucille Lang Day, author of *Birds of San Pancho and Other Poems of Place*, coeditor of *Fire and Rain: Ecopoetry of California*

Naomi does a wonderful job weaving together her dreams, her family, her heritage, Jung, Lorca – and they all seem to inform her rich and active imagination. The result is poetry that is as much a pleasure to read as it is engaging and tender. Each poem takes us on a journey where Naomi reveals a part of her life and, in so doing, she invites us along, not only to share her revelations but to inspire us to explore our own lives and impulses.

   – Stewart Florsheim, author of *A Split Second of Light*

I was thunderstruck by the raw power of *Death and His Lorca* – uttering of life, like prehistoric lava coming out from cavernous unknowns, turning unexpectedly into the finest weaving of fire strands mapping a life lived from the imaginal depths. The wisdom and the liberty of the Crone throws everything into the cauldron of transformation: the ordinary magic of early family life steeped in the archetypal adventures of the great-great-great grandparents, with the out-of-placeness of immigrant transits, the poignant remembrance of the refined father, the fading of the beloved mother destined to be taken by "The Shadow Sisters." Lowinsky revisits her first love and sees that it was impossible to fit all that made her the bard-shaman she became into the marriage: "cravings for what can't be measured", "the cave in which the unbearable brooded." The body poetic that laments the replaced hip that will not rest in the cave of the ancestors and the fairy-folk playing trickster-tricks in her breast. Nothing escapes the crone's Crazy Wisdom, the essence of each intensified mysterious moment, be it lived now or then, in wakefulness or in dream, on Mount Diablo or among the ghosts of the Mezquita de Cordoba: all the bones are in the broth, and one can almost taste the elixir, the fleshless, shimmering dancing particles that are Lila – the Dream.

– Alicia Torres, author *of Fatal* and *Regarding the Rose*

During a return to Spain – as visitor, as descendant of the exiled, seeking the resting place of Lorca – the poet reckons with loss, with aging, and with a host of shadows and various light, the relation between these the connections of one generation to another. Death, the poet says of Lorca, "has written you into everything," and the poet's Oma – having painted a portrait of herself in which her granddaughter later sees herself and her mother – is written to yet once again now that the poet is close in age to her grandmother at the time of the self-portrait. This moving collection reminds us how we find those who come before us and after by attending to what we see, what we dance, and what we create.

– Forrest Hamer, author of *Rift*, *Middle Ear* and *Call and Response*

DEATH AND HIS LORCA

Poems

Naomi Ruth Lowinsky

BLUE LIGHT PRESS ❖ 1ST WORLD PUBLISHING

SAN FRANCISCO ❖ FAIRFIELD ❖ DELHI

Death and His Lorca

BLUE LIGHT PRESS
www.bluelightpress.com
bluelightpress@aol.com

1ST WORLD PUBLISHING
PO Box 2211
Fairfield, IA 52556
www.1stworldpublishing.com

BOOK & COVER DESIGN
Melanie Gendron
melaniegendron999@gmail.com

COVER BACKGROUND PAINTING
"When Trees Go Wild,"
watercolor by Emma Hoffman (Oma)

INTERIOR ILLUSTRATIONS
Melanie Gendron

COVER PAINTING PHOTOGRAPHER
Ryan Bush

AUTHOR PHOTO
Dan Safran

FIRST EDITION

Library of Congress Cataloging-in-Publication Data

ISBN: 978-1-4218-3702-4

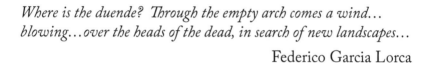

Where is the duende? Through the empty arch comes a wind…
blowing…over the heads of the dead, in search of new landscapes…

Federico Garcia Lorca

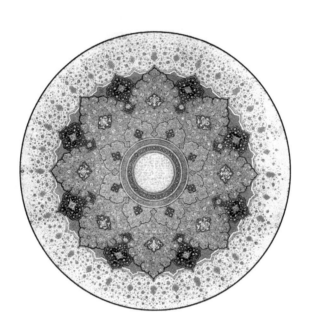

For Dan

my root

and my canopy

Table of Contents

Section Two: Your Spirit Inhabits My Bones

Section Three: Some Questions for the Dream Maker

Flamenco Dancer

When her arms rise up like Gaudi's spires
and her hands unfurl like forest violets
When the lamentation of the Moors   the Gypsies   the Jews
makes an agony about her eyes   and her spine
is a wild and supple snake   When she hitches up her skirts
and the stamping begins   in red shoes   She is riding
the exiled horse of her hips   over the yellow land
over dust that remembers   ashes of the burnt
bones of the broken   The soles of her feet
beat a drum   arousing the spirits   of her great
great   great   great   grand   parents

> She rides and she rides
> that exiled horse
> over Lorca's unmarked grave

I

Last Reckoning

I want to die my own death, by mouthfuls.

Federico Garcia Lorca

Tongue

Can do muscle of the mouth   A spit of land
into the sea   is made of flame   is made of flesh

Tolls the bell   Is used to signal lascivious intent   Has carnal
knowledge of a lover's mouth   When stuck out by a fierce

child means   *You are not the boss of me!*   Licks salt
if you're a deer   Hangs out on a hot day   if you're a dog

Leaps to the roof of your mouth when yelling   *Hallelujah!*
Tastes the hint of blackberry in the wine   When married

to groove creates a joint in the wood   Is sliced up and served
with Dijon mustard at a ladies   luncheon ca 1955

Is gotten by the cat   tied   twisted   Can give a lashing   tell
terrible truths   big lies   spill the beans   Speaks for the unseen

the hurt embattled heart   the lonely mind keeping watch
on the parapet   Consider how many have been cut out

by the slave master   lost to the bulldozer in the rain forest
to the mining company that cuts off the top of mountains

whole theogonies   creation stories   lineages   long gone
this fleshly messenger   Only the bony grin of teeth   remains

Córdoba Haunts Me

All night the ringing of the doorbell   Has someone
forgotten their keys?   Is Lorca's ghost in town?
Perhaps it's the poet Wallada   taunting my sleep
chanting her provocations   in Arabic
across nine centuries

Ding dong the bell   Each time an unseen
guest   a poltergeist is ringing   Dan
is rational   Maimonides is his man   He times
the bell   Once a minute   Once every two
minutes   His theory   a battery is dying   slowly

Jung is my man   The dead have arrived
on their way to Jerusalem   on their way to Mecca   They ring
and ring   here in the city of moaning doves   where three sons
of Abraham   once cultivated each other's gardens
There are as many ghosts here   as there are pillars

in the Mesquita   as many ghosts as there are red and white
arches   hanging lamps   luminous mosaics   points of light
emptiness in the Maqsura   where longing is carved
into stone   As many ghosts as there are interloping stained
glass windows   weeping saints   painted virgins

As many ghosts as there are phantoms murmuring
in the synagogue   I hear them   feel the density
of their prayer   They pray for peace
in Jerusalem   for peace in me   O fountains of the gone
arabesques of exile   city of the burnt   and the forbidden
                                        Remember us

When I'm Gone

Who will remember a girl's crush
on Adlai Stevenson?   The earnest precinct

walks   the beloved silver lapel
pin   a shoe with a hole in its sole

meaning eggheads are loveable   Remember Einstein's
mismatched socks?   Who will remember

the violet glow of Oma's eyes
telling tales of Erich   the dying tiger

in the Berlin Zoo   his throaty greeting
each time she came to paint him   before she knew

she was marked a Jew   Who will remember
how safe it seemed in America?   The war was won

the streets were calm   a child could play
Cowboys and Indians all day until dusk

How green the lawns   how sweet the smell
of honeysuckle   before the House UnAmerican

Committee   before billy clubs and dogs   before
four little girls in church

before Howl?

Who will remember her skinny
little girls' body   before breasts had their way

and nothing was safe anymore?

Venus Transit

You who've been
bound to me

by the memorabilia
of first love

first tongue in my mouth
first hand on my breast

are the first of us
to be snatched

ripped out of body
flung out of spring

while Venus makes
her rare transit

across the face
of the sun

It's been a lifetime
since Venus undid

our bonds
but you're touching me now

There's no more
pretending

that sneak thief
only visits others

You are back

my awakener

Last Reckoning

In the time of apricots   the moon   which was never
your thing   grows huge   enfolding you
in white light   I've come to visit
your final bed   in Rm. 618   with its long view

of the Berkeley hills   the Campanile   You
the first to touch me   in the dark Chevy
in the Eucalyptus grove   tell me your body's
last reckoning   Even now you are so

rational   test results   blood numbers   You shrug
If it would make any difference   you'd let them
fill you up with toxic chemicals   again   There's no way out
you say   but out   Your matter-of-fact surrender

touches me   Your crucible of white light
dazzles me   Our daughters touch your face
look into your eyes   Our son holds on
to your hand   How many seasons of apricots

since I slipped out of your bed   You never could reckon why
The moon which swallows mountains   decades
the Ganges   where once we stood with our children
watching corpses burn   shines on our son   age 6

who announced   "When you die it's I
who'll light your funeral pyre"   I see you sliding
into white water   Your angel   did you know
you have one?   is beckoning

There's no more reckoning
                              between us

5

I'm Sorry

the silver fish that once leapt
between us
never found words

Sorry there was never a fireplace
for the flame that flared
before ashes

Sorry my cravings for what
can't be measured   weighed   quantified
found no chalice   no pot on the stove

in that tiny med school apartment
where you studied chemistry
and I read Doctor Zhivago

Sorry I had no words
for the cave in which
the unbearable brooded

I needed a walk in the redwoods
shimmer of light on our faces
You needed to drive to the Ace hardware

for batteries
Once I walked around Stow Lake
two guys in a rowboat flirted with me

I wanted to run away with them
One day I did
I'm not sorry

I became such a house on fire
such a snake
in the summer grasses

I am sorry it's taken me
past your death
you wandering

the unknowable
without fireplace
without batteries

me chanting in Tibetan
for forty-nine days   while
the unbearable brooded

to remember
that silver fish

Ghazal in Your Wake

for Barbara

Your candle gutters on the kitchen counter   So shaken your
                                        song without words
The firestorm that took you   savaged us all   Soul shudders   a
                                        dirge without words

A camel shaped thunderhead carries you off to the furthest
                                        rim of the world
Spirit sputters   at the edge of abyss   Where goes your song
                                        without words?

You keep me kitchen company   It wasn't always easy   You
                                Dan's ex   me his second wife
Awkward edges irritated mutters all simmered away in our tribal
                stew   We brewed us a song without words

You greet me in the predawn dark   It's winter solstice   not
                                yet a week you've been gone
Flame flutters   You are the rain in the naked trees   Song of
                                the river   without words

Walking by the canal   where he's only ever seen ducks   Dan
                                beholds You rising
in the form of an egret   Utter wonder   Your splendid wings
                                Your song without words

Sitting shiva   so many friends   so much food   so many stories
                                        Shutters open
How little I knew of your big shining life   A chorus is singing
                                your song   without words

Your daughters wear your glamorous threads   Your son hasn't
shaved since you died

8

Just weeks ago they were all in your bed   a clutter of photos   a
clutch of memories
                                So haunted   your song without words

No wig for you   You shaved all that lustrous hair   I admired
your bald head   your fuchsia beret   your leopard print pants
So bold a rebutter of the one with the scythe   So fierce   your
                                                song without words

Your flame has burnt out   I miss you   Once you were a master
                                                flower cutter
an elegant arranger   I fill your empty candle jar with gemstone
                                        roses   garnet   coral   topaz
They sing you a song without words

You've changed   out of your vivid jewel tones   into muted gray
                                blues   mist on the mountain
I Naomi   your kin by long second marriage   pour sweet butter
                        on your name   Barbara   Bless   your thin air
                                        the song of your life

                                                Beyond words

9

Shades of the Gathered and the Gone

When your closed eyes see
　　　　　　the faces of the dead
When their resurrected bodies do
　　　　　　　a dance
around the bedroom floor
　　　　　　Do you know who speaks
while the moon goes about
　　　　　　her extravagant business
and you're worlds away
　　　　　　from the traffic of morning?

A long gone father reaches out
　　　　　　what was his arm
If only he could touch
　　　　　　your life once more
Have you figured out
　　　　　　what is required
when wild women
　　　　　　in wine red　　in druid green
come running through the woods
　　　　　　blood on their hands?

Do you know which god it is
　　　　　　among the elders by the sea
who sent those breezes
　　　　　　so the golden ships of Troy
could sail into your dream
　　　　　　bleed through　into your day?

If a Dream Could Change the Story

I'd remember joy between me and my father
as there was in his face when he played
with my little grandson   in last night's dream
The light in his eyes   would have filled the cells
of my brothers' bodies   and they would be glad men now

My father was more interested in illuminated
manuscripts   than in the play of little boys
They'd get rowdy   he'd storm out of his study
hurl thunderwords   rain rage upon my brothers'
heads   where it lives to this day

If a dream could change the story   I'd be as easy
in the company of my father's Bonnie as I was
in last night's dream   but my father's father
had a Bonnie too   and the family cloth's been ripped
in the name of my grandmother   in the name of my mother

If a child can engender a fabulous dream
it must have happened just the other night
when my four year old grandson
sat on his potty and tried
to piece together the story

"When my mommy was a little girl
did she live with you and grandpa Dan?
Where was her daddy Barry?"   The rips
and tears in my daughter's heart   in mine
are pored over by this half naked
little one   keeping me talking

so he won't have to lie down in his bed
all alone   My mother has slept alone for years
Grandpa Barry sleeps with his second wife
My father's Bonnie sleeps with her second husband
His father's Bonnie   long gone into the dance of light

and dark matter   is one with my father's
long gone mother   one with the singers of the song
I sing to the child of my child   my father sang to me
his mother sang to him about birds in the woods and golden rings
                                        If only he'd go to sleep

About Our Father

And Esau hated Jacob
Genesis

The quarrel between us is
as old as the bible

Who got his blessing?
Who got the back of his hand?

Come sit with me
Remember the land

we believed in as children?
The money we collected in tins

for trees in the desert? We believed
we would lay down our weapons

we would each have a vineyard
an olive tree a dove

> *Your Jerusalem has never been*
> *my Jerusalem*

The quarrel between us is
as old as the bible

Decrescendo of a Musicologist

He had no time for this
hospital room   this sour
bed   that jackass president

talking Star Wars on TV   No stomach
for secret arms deals   the cancer
his doctors insisted was eating

him   No stomach for his daughter's
eyes   her foolish talk
of love   He had important work

to complete   He was the only one
who understood
the modulations of the Renaissance

motet   the secret underneath
the music   its covert passageways
to freedom   He had no time

to remember   the midnight border crossing
out of Germany   the glittering
northern light under the bridges

of Amsterdam   the sun drenched
bougainvillea gracing the houses
of Havana   those impossible days

in New York City   when even the Musicians

Emergency Fund could not find him
a job   while his mother

lay dying at Lag Westerbork and he
was on his very important way
to Gloria   to Exaltate   to a many throated Amen

forever arguing with that critic
who claimed he had no facts to back up
his theory of secret modulations

on the way to freedom   Where was the tribute
for his scholarly rigor   precise
as a physics experiment?   Where the tribute

for his sweeping vision?   Who but he
could trace a mystical chromaticism
from Hebraic melodies in Spain

to Gregorian Chant in Italy   to the motet
in the Netherlands   to spirituals
sung by slaves in the American South?

Hadn't he served Lady Liberty?
Hadn't he followed the siren song
of Venus?   His ears left

the rest of him   wandered away   They had no stomach
for all this noise   Star Wars   the clash
of bedpans   those indecent

beeping machines   all this Sturm
und Drang which threatened
to drown out   he could almost hear it   the music

of the spheres   Where
had his daughter gone?   What was it
she'd been saying?

Your People Are My People

For Al Young

My people are the people of the pianoforte and the violin
Mozart people   Bach people   Hallelujah people
My people are the Requiem people   Winterreise people   Messiah
people   who crossed the red sea   Pharoah's dogs
                                    at our heels

Your people are the drum beat people   the field holler people
the conjure people   Blues people   Jubilee people   people who
talk straight to God   Your people are the Old Man River people
the Drinking Gourd people   singing the Lord's song
                                    in a strange land

My family had a Sabbath ritual
We lit the candles sang Go Down Moses   sang Swing Low
Sweet Chariot   sang slave music freedom music secret signals
in the night music   My father said you never know
                                    when Pharoah will be back

I was young
I was American   I thought
my people were the Beatles   the Lovin' Spoonful   the Jefferson
Airplane   singing Alice and her White Rabbit through all
                those changes my parents did not understand

That didn't last
That was leaving home music   magic mushroom music
Puff the Dragon music   floating off
to Never Never land   now heard in elevators
in the pyramids of finance

But Old Man River still rolls through my fields
Bessie Smith still sweetens my bowl
Ma Rainey appears in the inner sanctum
of the CG Jung Institute   flaunting her deep black bottom

My father's long gone over Jordan
and I'd hate for him to see
how right he was about Pharoah

but I want you to know   Al
every Christmas
in black churches all over Chicago
the Messiah shows up
accompanied by my mother's
        Hallelujah violin

New Hat for the Dreamer

If your father   who used to be bald   shows up in the dream
in the form of your son when the chaos has got him

If his hair's gone berserk like the bad boy in the German
children's book who never cuts his hair or his nails

If he's pale and weird
a walking disaster   a hungry ghost

what hat should you be wearing?
In the dream you are given an American hat

made of straw with long red ribbons
Everyone loves it

If your job in the dream is to sing a lullaby
to your father who is your son who is a hungry ghost

who walks on your grave   If your job is to rock him
in the bosom of Abraham   as your father rocked you

as you rocked your son and sang
about handing over your soul to Gott or God

or whatever you call the hungry father of the night
who may or may not return it   come morning

Would an American hat of straw with long red ribbons
a little girl in spring kind of hat
make any difference?

Lullaby of Lineage

If only I knew how to ride a melody
backwards in time

I'd visit my father in Stuttgart   a hundred years ago
He's four

He's wandered into the music room
with that dreamy look I remember

His mother stands in the doorway
watching a ray of light

touch his face   She's so enchanted
by her son   how green his eyes

how delicate his fingers and his bones
That melody in minor mode   he picks out

on the keys   is that the lullaby
she used to sing to him   If I could be

a particle of light   one of the dust motes
floating about this family of Russian Jews

recently escaped from Pale and pogrom
If I could linger in this moment   taste its sweetness

before the First War   before the Second War
before Rachel weeps for her children again

Surely I could find my way to you
daughter of the daughter of my daughter's son

once I have slipped out of flesh
into the dance of particles

a hundred years from now
I could be a dust mote in a ray of light

touching you   your hands on your belly
in that gesture I'll remember

from when I had a body
Surely you will feel me   your agitated ancestor

wanting to know you have survived
floods   fires   famine   wanderings to higher ground

I'll wish I had a human voice to sing to you
that old lullaby   played by my father

on the piano   in minor mode
when he was four

Speaking Truth to Trickster

Every time I make myself a world

> you
> throw a rock
> a window shatters

Every time I think I've figured it out

> this is my house
> this is how I make money
> this is how I make dinner

the rice burns
the market plunges
the house shape-shifts   into a down–
        hill camel

> I'm no Bedouin

What do I know
        of tents   of sand?

I had a many-storied world

> It floated off   like a box kite

You say   "Forget how it was
Make something
new   Use
your imagination"   I imagine

you as camel boy

> *Take the long toothed beast*
> *by the mouth   though*
> *He'll spit*
> *Lead us both   to water*

Death and His Lorca

You were always with him
etched in the mountains
slapping his face with a gust
      of terror   at night
      in the Albaicin
      where a gypsy might spirit
      his soul to a cave
      while his friends kept on
          laughing
          drinking
your icy fist in his guts
your minotaur shadow looming
          over the Moorish wall

You sang him a broken moon
You slipped him the knife at the wedding
You entered his dream spitting teeth
Why couldn't you have let him have
his life   while he had it?

Death, this is your country
      Yours the Auto da Fe
      Yours the synagogue's ghosts
      Yours the ruins at Madina al-Zahra

And Lorca
he's written you into everything
his end always known to his beginnings
      as fire knows its ash
      as blood knows the heart's final shudder…

II

Your Spirit Inhabits My Bones

*They loot Last Night. They hug old graves, root up
Decomposition, warm it with a kiss.*

Gwendolyn Brooks

News from the Dead

The dead are back   with stories
I haven't heard   with letters found
in the attic   behind the winter clothes

They're worried about their Haitian
passports   (German Jews
with Haitian passports?)   The letters say

they cannot be renewed   They're citizens
of nowhere   My grandfather's calm
and competent hands are trembling   Suppose

the government declares them enemy
aliens?   They knock on closed doors   insist
on seeing the vice consul   himself

In the world they left me   Beethoven's hands
are all over the piano   The "Still Life with Persian Melon
and Black Grapes"   my grandmother painted

before I was even imagined
comforts me   Suppose I could eat
those grapes   taste the lush light

of a late German summer   breathe the air
of that storied house   The dogs
would be sleeping   the parrot be perched

on my mother's young shoulder   singing
"Povero Rigoletto"   Would the dead   relieved
of their need for passports   settle down
                                    and go back to sleep?

Moon Lamentation

your ashen hair Shulamith we shovel a grave in the air
Paul Celan

Lady of silvery light   *Do not forget her*
She wears a glittering gown   strokes our faces

We've planted a tree for her   in the Promised Land

Lady of waning light   *Do not forget her*
A mother of Israel   lays her head on the coffin

Ice cream parlor   summer night   suicide bomber
A father of Palestine stands

on a hill   His daughter
gathers apricots near the border   He sees it all

the pursuit of a runaway lamb   a tank   a shot

where not so long ago her grandfather

tended the olive groves
Lady of lost light   our bride of the dark

Her spirit is wandering
where olive trees have been torn by the roots

Do not forget her

I See You in the Foothills Oma

I wear you like a necklace with one lost stone
I feel you in my bones   in the slow dance of the vineyards
in the violet hills   their meander to the edge of sky
In mirrors your nose is my nose
Your spirit inhabits my eyes

You're with me in the foothills   the wine country
My husband manages maps   reservations
while you carry on   in English   in German
about shades of mauve   of purple   of green
It's my birthday   I'm as old as you were

when I was the age of my grandson   He's 10
And I suddenly need to know   what happened to you
when your husband   who managed visas   investments
who got most of the family out of Europe
dropped dead one afternoon   the smell from the ovens

fresh in his nose   and me just born?   How is it
I never asked?   Did colors ebb
from the sky?   Did your spirit sink
to the dark below roots?
You were so new to this far west   so far

from all you knew   with 25 years still to go
vineyards to paint and mountains and me
Your daughter   my mother   can no longer find her way
from yesterday to tomorrow   Who will complete the story?
I wear you like a necklace with one lost stone

There is no place on earth where you don't see me
Your spirit inhabits my bones

A Grandmother's Self–Portrait Speaks

Flesh is my home
Flesh   brief as it is   my consolation
I could have painted blue horses   gone galloping off
into the unseen   I could have rendered the wings
of violins or dazzled your eyes with blazes of geometry

Even my own Corinth   who taught me to follow the light
went wandering off into inner life
breaking it off with Rembrandt   Franz Hals   Courbet
He told me my work was
overly domesticated   Why not?
given that I was to lose
a daughter   two sons   a home   a country

Flesh is my sanctuary
and my communion with you
Generations after the paint has dried
you pull me out of the closet
you need to see me again
to mirror my fierce focus
the unbearable set of my mouth
the North Sea light as it falls on my face
the loosening skin of my neck

What aspect of you do you seek in my eyes?

Notice my palette is dark
I use light and shadow
to define my decline
Behind me divided worlds   the hard edge
of studio wall   and the glow
from the unknown side   that blue green whimsy
where breeze stirs the curtains
where your eyes go

Brown on Brown

The Netherlands   1934

Brown is the color of ache
Brown and a touch of orange
renders my Low Country brooding
in water color

Everything hangs in the air
land   water   dikes
somebody's drifting house
my dead   my dread

Brown is the mother of longing
Brown is the mother of blood and its stains
Brown is this sepia daydream
this monochromatic mood

I sit by my window reflecting
on brown and its shades of pale
Watercolor won't hold back the tide
nor will the dikes

only brown
and the slenderest brush I can find
only my wistful
sky reaching strokes

Say trees
Say roots
Say someday
maybe leaves

Only the Snow Knows

Kassel, Germany 1931

There are no more tears
Only the broken trees
Only the neighbor's house in horror
at its cold dead load

Only the snow knows
where they've gone
into what black mouth

Everything is agitated
Agitated windows
Agitated walkways
Agitated brush strokes

Spirit leaks into earth

Only the snow knows
where they've gone
your sons in the land   beyond sun

Everything is torn
Limbs from trees
Heart from house
An agony of oil paint
gouges the sky

Only the snow knows
the treachery of mountains
There are no more tears

When Trees Go Wild

The Netherlands   1938

They wander no man's land
  With suspicious passports
    They clothe themselves in ghost fire
      Orange flames   green flames

They forget they belong to the ground
  They deny the skies
    They leap into waters where war lurks
      With crocodile teeth

If we ran we would lose our roots
  If we stayed we'd be chopped
    Into kindling
      For the mad man's fire

If our spirits could rise and perch
  In the canopy   like jungle birds
    Like souls of a different persuasion
      Yoruba let's say

We might dance ourselves into trance
  But be lost to our dead
    Forgotten by stones
      By bodies of water

When trees go wild
  They burn orange and green in water
    They dive in the dark where war lurks
      With crocodile teeth

Until They Let the Jews into America

Cuba 1939

We're stuck on this island   where I am
a stranger to myself   Where ground
goes slant   Where sun is

a sorcerer   I've no idea
how they live in that hut   How
do they cook?   How

do they wash?   Who
sleeps with whom?   Even the palms
lean North   lest they lose

their balance   Lest red run riot
Lest flowers and drum unravel
my mind   Lest my eye be lured

into deep dark   where jungle gods dance
Lest I lose my Bach
Lest my Schubert forget

his winter journey
Lest my name   written in grass   wither
under the eyes of that sorcerer   the sun

Refuge

I'm here
Footstep and breath
Real as the trees
Real as the archway they make
from shadow to glow
Real as my painting in oil
for your eyes

Trees are my rock and my roots
Trees are my silent angels
Will the ghosts ever find me?
Will they build their nests in these branches
Here
as they did in Europe?

> We are refugees from that room
> with its single bare light bulb
> Will our visas ever be granted?
> Will our dead know where we've gone?

I'm here
Heartbeat and belly
Real as the woman I paint
passing through shade into glow
hungry for sun and the sea
and for you yet to be

I'm here
Belly and breath
Trees are my rock and my temple
Trees are my vigilant angels
And you   soon to be

will you make your nest here?

Portrait of the Girl I Was   Age 14

Although I don't enjoy
looking at you   a clogged life
in a white dress   holding red flowers

(Oma must have thrust
those blood blooms
into your haunted hands)

Although you sit there   deer eyed
ready to bolt   *Cossacks will gallop through*
Nazis will kick in the door

Although the music's
gone underground   and you've lost
that wild horse you used to ride

Although you'll dream
of spitting broken teeth
into the road for years

before you learn
the sanctity
of your own red room

Although I've never noticed
this before   Behind your back
in a far corner

of canvas   there is an open
window   a hint
of radiance   a glimpse

of green trees
You can't see it yet   but
Oma has painted
your way out...

Your Creation

Self Portrait   Berkeley 1957/8

You have made yourself so self contained   Oma
singular   sage   Your left hand reaches beyond the frame for what
can't be seen   You have given yourself a white blouse   It sets off
your olive skin   You have given yourself a brooch   pinned
just so   I remember that brooch   You are haloed
in a flow of brush strokes   Touches of wine
pensive blue   tender yellow   all the soft shades
embrace you   For this moment it's all in balance   the light
you've gathered   the long stony story of all
you've surrendered   in oils   in water colors   You have made yourself

with your own knowing eyes   I remember them   You saw me
on the rag   seething at my father   stewing about my boyfriend
scared to be   You showed me the makings of a maker
vision   obsession   plodding perseverance   For this moment your
                                                        essence
takes form   Soon enough you'll begin your tumble   into that
                                                        torture chamber
you thought you'd buried   Your eyes will know me no more   I'll
                                                        leave you howling
at your nurses   You'll return to me   as ashes   But Oma   I have
                                                        written you
and I have written you and I have written you and here I am not far
from where you are in that self portrait   Writing you again

Grandmother Ghost in the Brush Strokes

Grandmother ghost in the brush strokes
Grandmother glow in the sky
Grandmother weeping willow
Grandmother breath of the mountain

Grandmother glow in the sky
Burning snake in the house
Grandmother breath of the mountain
Snake on fire in the grasses

Burning snake in the house
Nothing will be what it was
Snake on fire in the grasses
Fire between brother and brother

Nothing will be as it was
Ghosts are smoke and ashes
Fire between brother and sister
Mother has wandered away

Ghosts are ashes and brush strokes
How long do embers stay hot?
Mother has wandered away
How long will it be 'til spring?

How long do embers stay hot?
O grandmother weeping willow?
How long will it be 'til spring?
I gaze at your ghost in the brush strokes

Past Lives

Dark woods
my mother
lost
her childhood in

        those
        graves

Where is my grandmother's
        Spanish
            shawl?

        Where is the wolf?

If trees
stop speaking
perhaps   graves
        will

Listen

        every
        leaf
        a story

        Then comes
            the dream
                winter

You Who Studied Sorrow

You who studied sorrow in the mirror
You who could paint the sharp edge of joy
the uplift of mountains
tree light in lakes

Were you with me at the family reunion?
Were you with your last living child?
She was our central fire
Now she's 90

She flickers
She fades
She gets lost in the ashes
Can't remember why

we're all gathered around her
We bad blood
We furies stuffed
into zippered compartments

while the fire pit blazes

It's late
and the young ones are pounding
tequila shots   talking
blue moons

It's late
and their holy flares
light up the dark
even unto the fifth generation

It's late
And the one who did not come

troubles me   He's alone
in that dark motel room

contemplating
your watercolor birches
Black holes
eat the soles

of his feet
Will he ever
see his mother
again?

O you who could paint
the sharp edge of joy
You who studied sorrow
in the mirror

help me face mine

Elephant Child

a person is a person because of other people
African saying

We are a many–headed   land cruising   Toyota machine
a creature agog with zoom lenses

One of us sees her   the elephant child
playing alone   in a pool of water

"Is she alright?"   "Can we get closer?"   "Where
is her mother?"   From beyond

the corners of our eyes a sudden throng
Her grandmothers   her mother   her aunts

her baby cousins lumbering
across the road to save her from whatever

threat we might be   Their mission
dissolves into play   They spray

water on each other   They wallow   They throw mud
We watch

as they rise dark and glistening
so glorious in the late afternoon light

The little one who played alone   approaches
our Toyota   Holds up her sensitive trunk

She is trying to figure us out
We are trying to figure her out   Is she

a problem child   a soon to be leader
the future shaman of her clan?   Her mother

has had enough of her shenanigans
Herds her in close   as the sun begins to set

over the Chobe river valley
They stand touching

the big one
the little one

encircled by kin
We understand

An elephant is an elephant
because of other elephants

Root Canal

1. Security Line

We are pilgrims on our way to see Mother   among travelers
in flip flops   with Bluetooths   carrying babies   We walk
in our radiant bodies   One of us is about to crack

a tooth   Only the babies can see   old light
from past lives   Only the babies can hear
the song lines   We are pilgrims passing through

the metal detector   We remove our shoes   remove
our coats and shawls   Some of us will be hand wanded
silver bracelets   seven quarters   three dimes   provoke

the security gods   The Kennedy who just died
is speaking thirty years ago on TV   His assassinated
brothers still bleed into our lives

2. Retirement Living

In Mother's eighty-eighth year she got scammed   Sweet talkers
from the islands poured delirium into her ears   drained her purse
A Great Lake swimmer lost face   A late Beethoven violin

bowed to the gods of security   We've come
to see her new place among the formerly eminent
Hyde Park intellectuals   We walk the round of her days   She

gets lost   Forgets her song lines   Wants to sort through
scores of Mozart   Bartok   Bach   What goes where?   The
                                        Kennedy who died

is talking on TV   It's his funeral   His widow pushes back her
dark

hair   She's known him on her belly   in her thighs   She knows
his secret smell   When is it my tooth cracks?
When does that big bully nerve take over?

3. Roots

Oma's paintings dominate this place   She painted
herself painting all her ages   painted herself losing
her grip   She looked straight into her own mirrored eyes

and painted the edge of her nerve   We make a pilgrimage
to see her painting of German snow on roofs in 1931
the naked larches scrape the sky   Her sons are dead

Her sons are dead   Her sons are dead   Trees
save her   Trees leaf   Trees bud   Trees flower
Trees know her secret smell   They cleanse her dreams

Trees grow by rivers   by canals   by lakes   They reflect
on themselves in oils   in watercolors   They burn orange
in the deep wood   They burn gold under water   Mother loses track

of the song lines of her Mother   Her brothers bleed
into brothers not yet born   Mother says we live
too far away   that we've been swallowed by the State of California

4. Going Home

I am losing my own grip   My finger prints fade   I forget
your name   All I know is the scream of a nerve   I've no idea
how the widow got into Mother's TV   no idea

how an endodontist removes a dying nerve   no idea
how a plane leaves this earth   no idea
how I'll live in the State of California
                              while Mother loses track of herself

At Nineteen   Before She Became My Mother

Havana   1939

I still like to play with my sisters   even
when we're cooking   cleaning   making
the beds   how quickly we can make
each other laugh   When we go out
in the afternoon   after the worst

of the heat   to take photographs
of palm trees   dark skinned
people   how bananas grow
I skip like a school girl   in my summer
dress   surprised to find us all

alive   on this tropical island
in a bright blue ocean   far
from the grim trains   the grieving
skies of northern
Europe   Is it really me

who is the first of three sisters
to be married?   Is he really
mine   the elegant man in the panama
hat   the light summer suit   playing
piano accompaniment to my mother's

melancholy Schubert lieder?
You wouldn't believe how
seriously he can speak   on and on
about the flow of light and shadow
in the portrait my mother is painting

of my sister in white among
flowers   It makes me giggle
Is it really me whom he sends
those tender looks across the dining
room table   where we sit with the rabbi

and talk about Moses   the wandering
tribes of Israel   Is it really me
in the night   when he makes it magic
soft touch of his fingers   sweet
whisperings   Will it really be me

when we get to the promised
land   Will I live
far from my parents   Will I really
be his   American wife and bear him
                              American children?

Mother Approaches the Border

Mother is leaving us
slow step by slow
                lingering step

She's ascending the winter trees
             without bud
             without leaf

She looks back
            a runaway child
            without overcoat

Time is a broken necklace
She's given up gathering
             spilt beads

Yesterday
is a clanging
in the basement pipes

Tomorrow chugs down the track
blowing its horn   Where
             are her sisters?

Who has the passports?
Must she cross
the border alone?

The lake's in a bad
weather mood
Snowflakes lick her cheeks

Mother laughs at the ducks
how they dive into what
                  we can't see

She has nowhere to go
                but up
tending the business of sky

She has nowhere to go
                but down
having settled

the questions
             of dust
             of ashes

She doesn't belong to us anymore
She belongs to the naked trees
to the lake and its bad weather mood

to the ducks diving into what
                  we can't see

Mother   Between Now and the Dark

Those Sisters with Scissors poke holes in you
Cut out tomorrow   Dismember yesterday
Entangle your yarn 'til you don't know who
    you are or where

You lose the bathroom or it loses you
as if you hadn't just been there
I show you down my brother's
                    long corridor

past your mother's final
self portrait   You wheel
your walker back to me   your daughter
               from California

     I see me on the potty chair
     you perched on the bathtub chanting
             "spss spss spss spss"

You sit at table   Refuse your juice   Refuse
your tuna salad   I hear your voice in my childhood
"Eat a little   drink a little"   "My voice?" you marvel
                 A sudden shift of light

Your gaze meets mine
"I wonder what you'll write about me now?"
For this moment you know me   even here in Indiana

'til the Shadow Sisters steal
your face from me   O I regret
the half a continent between us   I regret

I must leave you again   You point
out the window into late autumn
Red leaves flame on the backyard maple
  "Look how beautiful"

As if you hadn't said that minutes ago
A sudden shift of light   and I too
can see the tree   As if

the Mother Daughter circle   still spins
As if those Scissor Sisters   aren't forever
                              lurking

Wrong Number

Nobody calls
in the night
Yanks me out
of a dream
Beats up my heart
Slashes my breath
Dashes my sweet
good sleep

Nobody rings
again
Dan picks up
No one
has nothing
to say

Nobody stalks me
in bed
Rattles my legs
Opens the door for
Skull mother

Skull mother reads
my palm
my stars
the irises of
my eyes
my round and round
my up and down
circling somebody's sun

Can she read
when I'll be
done?

Sunday Afternoon Phone Call

Mother doesn't know me anymore
My name has sunk
to the bottom of the pond

Mother doesn't know my voice

"To whom am I speaking?"
"I'm your daughter"
"You don't sound like her"

Mother has dropped her end

of the cord   I'm floating
in lonely space   Where
are my Mother's hands on my shoulders

making me stand up straight?

Where is her knowing laugh at how
I've got this all backwards   It's she
who is floating in unborn space

O Mother of the grain
I sit on your hard
hard rock   Talk bitters   to the gods

O Mother of the howling womb
Say No! to the green and the tender
Say No! to the hatchling and the bud

Say No! to the beat
that would move your feet

                    Music doesn't sing us anymore

Mother's Severed Head

Mother's severed head is talking in your sleep
All night long She's talking in tongues
Talking like there's no tomorrow

      Tomorrow has gone berserk
      Smashed tablets   hurled stones
      Terror breeds terror   & broken children

Look for Mother in memory   Look for Her in myth
in oak leaf   in river   in weeping willow
There's no sign of her body

      Chaos breeds chaos   & frightened children
      Coyote seizes the border
      Sex is traffic   Love is road kill

Once Mother worked for Chicago Child Care
Taught parenting skills to baby mamas
before blood crippled blood   before guns became God

Her body can't find Her head

      Mayhem breeds mayhem in the streets of Chicago
      Drug money kidnaps the kids of Honduras
      Sex is road kill   Gangs are God

Mother's in a rage about Oracle Arizona
How can a town whose name means Her shrine
Cast snake eyes on terrified children?

      Hate is a wild fire   It leaps across borders
      Gangs and guns ricochet
      What Jackal God eats babies?

Mother is a summons in the cave of dreams
Listen for Her wailing in the dark before the dawn
Wailing like there's no tomorrow

An American History Poem

Washington D.C.   January 2009

History is you and me
History is day and is night
          Wally Mongane Serote

Out of Africa
Out of Russia
Out of Ireland
Out of China
Out of El Salvador

History turns us inside out
History turns us around
We were slaves in Egypt
We were slaves in Mississippi
We clung to our roofs in the flooded Ninth Ward
We walked the trail of tears

By donkey cart
By night across borders
By raft
We children of the dark ship's hold

We who built the capital
were kept in cages
History turned us around
gave us another story

Beyond the rock in our bellies
Beyond the underground railway
History whispered liberty's secrets
We sang them loud

I am a Bill of Rights child
I am a black woman voter
I am the citizen daughter
of illegal aliens
who pick your apples

They came
They became
America

History rants and raves
History pulls out her hair
History is our mad maiden aunt
She lives in the attic
We don't want to hear her harangues

We saw Kennedy fall in that car
His bright blood on Jackie's suit
We saw Martin fall
      Robert fall
      Harvey Milk fall
A thousand freedom seekers murdered
                   in the jungle
We saw mountains decapitated
     Frogs gone
     Bees gone
     Fires
     Floods
In the shining city
     Homes are lost
     Citizens go hungry
     Lives hung out to dry
             on the bottom line

History spirals
History asks us to dance
We are gathered on the National Mall
We sit on the steps of the Lincoln Memorial
We are not the March on Washington
Not the Poor People's March
Not here to protest nor to petition
We organized
We walked the precincts
We voted to change America
We laugh
We weep
We update our face books
We tell stories of our ancestors
who longed for this day

We belong to the ones we came in with
We belong to each other
We dance in the cold winter sun
And even we who are caught
in the Purple Tunnel of Doom
                      know a glad ship's come in

Madelyn Dunham   Passing On

A wind blows when we die
For each of us owns a wind
            — Xan poem

I never knew I'd be wind   when I died   A warm wind
on my way home from the islands   A light breeze

off the lake   Breath in my grandson's lungs
as he speaks to the crowds on this

his election night   Does he know this is me
touching his face   and the faces of those who never believed

they'd see the day   Who'd have thought I'd be breath
in the bodies of so many strangers Who'd have thought I'd be music

sweet as the sound of the slack key guitar   or that I'd become
an ancestral spirit in the land where they know how to feed

the dead   They're roasting four bulls   sixteen chickens
some sheep and goats   to feast the one

who belongs to us all   To the Kenyan village
of his grandmother Sara   To the spirits of his father and mother
                                                his black

and white grandfathers   To the ones who are laughing and crying
in Grant Park   In the land of the dead   nothing is over

We still wander   still worry   take pleasure   make trouble   demand
                                                our portion
of beer   of drumming   of dancing all night   I say to you living

though I've drifted away   though I'm only a sigh   an ex–
halation   I can feel your whole world shift

though I'm only the faraway sound
                          of a slack key guitar...

Ghost Note for Persia

My sweet old beloved
from the days when I was
a Persian   unknown to you
but sung by the singers
of songs   who yearned
for jeweled skies   for flowering trees
in the gardens of so
long ago   Listen to me

my beloved mosaic   my miniature
of ladies whose horses have stopped
for a drink by the stream

There are worlds within worlds
the shouting   the war cries are dust   on the wind
We sit in the garden   A crescent moon sings

III

Some Questions for the Dream Maker

My whole life has been an altar
worth its ending.

Audre Lorde

The Shekhinah in Córdoba

In the sound of an early morning toilet flush
in the voices of fishmongers opening the market
in the door bell again   Who rings?
The bride of Sabbath arrives

How long since she's showed up
in a bed in Córdoba   wound her legs around
her love   tasted first light?

The doves have stopped moaning lamentations
Now it's honey-basted flesh
sweet fire of the loins   thigh music

O gatherer of dreams
Oranges are your harvest
                    and purple grapes

Some Questions for the Dream Maker

Why   in the dream drama
do you cast me in such
a nasty role?   Force me to force
a daughter of Atatürk   out
of her family mansion in Istanbul?   She

with the free flowing hair   Me
turned collaborator   with my old foe   the patriarch
who would claim   in my name   her Ottoman inheritance
Istanbul?   I've never even been to Istanbul
And the young woman   I'm on her side   Or

Is there an Istanbul within me?   A city of long ago
glory   An old lady city
whose empires have crumbled
whose melancholy clings to aging dwellings
Is there a dark–eyed young woman within me

pushed out of privilege   lost to her stars
gazing at the Bosporus through what used to be
her window   Where can she go?   There's turmoil
in the streets   There's war next door   A tyrant who murders
his own people   Refugees flood the borders

This is an old story   I think of my own
dark–eyed mother   cast out of childhood
sent wandering from world to world
with false papers   Who invaded her
many storied home   before it was bombed?

Our lady of Istanbul charms me   Offers me wine
from her father's cellar   Shows me her grandmother's library
books I know well   on the unearthed goddess   "Your goddess"
                                                    she says
"is my goddess"   It is dusk   We sit among sepia photographs
She wants us to live here together   inherit each other's ghosts

Doesn't she know what they do to collaborators?

Dream maker   if this is high drama
meant to reveal what I can't comprehend

                    Couldn't you turn up the lights?

The Angel of Rot

The roof rat does what roof rats do
crawls into the pipes under the sink
and dies   The smell of his death

takes dominion   We can't find
his body   We can't liberate
his corpse   The smell

of his death is master
in this house   bigger than
grandchildren coming for tea   bigger than

Uncle Solomon going to pot
in a shit motel in the valley   In Haiti
the earth opens up her alligator jaws and swallows

hundreds of thousands   The smell of their death
is bigger than the island   bigger
than the news on TV   Buddha sits

in the kitchen window   looking inward
Even Buddha can't clear his head
despite incense   despite hand

made beeswax candles   the rat stinks
The poet invokes the sweet smell
of night blooming jasmine   an Arabian garden

a peacock shrieks   The rat stinks   He
who has left us his body   looks down upon us
and smiles   For he is the angel of rot   He
will be Master

All Night Long I Track the Signs

We're in the dark again   on uneven ground   where only shad-
ows know the way   Your breath is my compass   Your hand
is the North Star   What have we stumbled into?   Stag's
skull crowns a tent of bones   We are to sleep here

Remember the stag in Ashland?   We stared at him through
window glass   He stared at us   especially you   May the
spirit of stag fill you with forest lore   How to leap over
thickets   blend into trees   lose the predator   lose antlers
grow new ones in spring

Something burrows below   rooting about in what we can't
fathom   A badger leaps out of the dark   Bites your neck
Claws your chest   I try to scream but can only stammer   If
this is a dream wake me   If this is a fairy tale send in the
woodsman   If this is my shadow I'll strangle him

In the world before you Wolf Man reigned   He huffed   he
puffed   he blew my house down   In the world of your love
I am held all night long   In the world beyond will you know
my face   my name?

Seeking sleep in a circle of bones   I hear you breathe   I
touch your hand

Down–Going River Song

Red River sing us a drinking song
Summer's spell   broken

Sing of the way we used to be
When we swam in each other

swam in you   Before
drought exhausted the garden   Before

fate rode in
on a Night Mare

> *Breath labors*
> *Blood stammers*

> *Bone is pierced*
> *to marrow*

> *Who let the mutant into the brew?*
> *Who turned the white light on?*

Red River sing of the down–going
Fierce feathers pierce the veil

What lurks around the bend?
Jungle?   Narrows?   Falls?

Will we be swept out to sea?

Will we rise as mist?
Fall as rain?

Red River
                Sing us

First Infusion

"I'm a green and yellow basket case" you tell me   shuffling
from bathroom to bedroom and back   We lean on each other
laughing   The basket weaver of the stars sent you to me   my
green man   my pollen   my salmon leaping up river   A tisket
a tasket   we're in the woods without a basket   Bear tracks
you   Badger bites your neck   draws bad blood   A gang of
cells gone rogue   steals your breath   your thunder   The world
unravels

We walk on narrow girders   afraid of the black hole beneath
We sit in the ribcage of a beached whale   look out to sea
through an arch of bones   You who always know the sun's
direction   have lost your bearings   Your body will not suffer
this infusion gladly   A horde of stranger antibodies   Who
let the barbarians in?

Here comes the old man of the woods   He knocks on the
roots of trees   He shuffles the seed waking dance of the bear
Here comes your Earth Soul   She's one of the weird sisters
wears dark skirts   keeps company with the owlet on her
shoulder   She and her owlet know all about rogue cells   all
about infusions   They work in your dark   weaving the forest
into your basket   tooth of badger   cave of bear   deep sleep of
late November

Here comes the rain   Here comes the great white egret
spreading its wings over us both as we leave the infusion center
The wild ones in the woods aren't done with you yet
Nor am I

The Russian Woman's Daughter

"The Russian woman's daughter is sweeping the floor" you
announce   hauling yourself out of chemo's last slime before
slipping back down into undertow   In dreams you are forever
travelling   driving near cliff's edge   navigating bus stops
running to catch a plane   Perhaps you're at a wedding in the
Old Country   where our dead have gathered to bless
the unknown bride   the unseen groom

Surely there's a grandmother who'll make you a big bowl of
borscht   Red root broth to purge you of aches   shakes   nasty
aggravations in delicate places   Surely they'll be gone like the
crumbs swept away by the Russian woman's daughter   Perhaps
it's her wedding   And the groom   I can see him now   dancing
in the glow of those who came before   aroused as the Green
Man in May

Here   in the Old Country of the Heart   you are my root and my
canopy   Here   in the garden   the earth's been turned   the seed-
lings planted   Come back to the river with me   Come back to
the farmer's market   Strawberries sing the sun's hot tongue   A
fiddler frolics a Klezmer tune   Our dead do a circle dance around
us   throw us high to the canopy sky

Angel of the Not Yet Known

Something is trying to be known
in a city whose language escapes me
in the unseeing eyes of the angel
his golden spots   the book he reads
the crowd that forms around him
taking photos   Something is trying to be
seen   in a corner of my mind   a sudden
flash   a turbulence of clouds   threat
of rain   Something is trying to be heard
on street corners where I wait
for word   A gust of wind disturbs
the palms   Crack
of thunder   Flurry
among shoppers descending
                    into the underground

Coming back through the Barri Gothica in the rain
the unformed not yet known
flutters   wet wings
The glowing bellies
of young women are
              a revelation   almost
                          to the pubic bone

Translations from Childhood

There is a line on the inside of a bent knee
This caused my brothers to explode
with laughter   I never knew

what this was code for
since "African Jungle" was their name
for our mother's dark

underbrush   out of which it was said
we'd emerged   My brothers snickered
my father's voice rose

Potfadorry! Jetzt hab ich aber eine Wut!

I tried to stay above this
talking Adlai Stevenson
buttermilk dressing

putting my sorry body
my agony eyes between
my father's hands   my brothers'

provocations   Did that prevent him
from knocking their heads together
from giving each an "Ohr Feige?"

I never learned what
"Potfadorry" means   Perhaps
it is a warrior call to rouse

the blood   I know that "Wut"
is hotter and nastier
than anger   I know an "Ohr Feige"

is an ear fig   To avoid it   I hid
behind a fig leaf   and watched
                    that serpent raise   his head

Exodus

Maybe I stutter
Maybe I can't get my tongue and my fire together
There's a burning bush that speaks to me
It is never consumed

You   my brother   are a fire
that can't be contained   Burning mad
that communism failed   Enraged
at those pigs on the right
Those cowering dogs on the left
And The People   all idiots
          bowing their heads
          in iPhone obsession

It burns you up   the whole catastrophe
Our father who smashed our heads together
Our mother who's wandered away
And then there's me   with my birds' nest obsessions
My rabbit holes   my sacred oak
I'd rather listen to mystical underbrush
than hear you rant

Maybe I stutter
Maybe I can't get my tongue and my fire together
But I know when to fold the tents
          and travel alone
                    to the mountain

Sometimes   Before First Light

I hear hobgoblin music   elf lyre   fairie fiddling   banshee harpist
plucking every note of dread out of a slow dawn   My right breast
could be harboring an enemy   The doctor points to a suspicious
shadow on his imaging machine   amidst galaxies of magnified
crushed flesh   This shadow   in the shape of a cigar   is just the
size an elf might smoke   while dreaming up a trick to play upon a
body trying to get back to sleep

The music turns processional   I'm in a tribe of elfin folk
proceeding gravely to the central fire   The Mother of the
Mountain takes my hand   Tongues lick the dark   A carved mask
appears   eyes and mouth aflame   *Don't you see?   It burns but is
not consumed?*   She kisses me full on the mouth   Is this Her
claim on me?   Her blessing?   The beginning of   my end?

Breast aches   Stomach lurches   Heart speaks   Steady old
girl   Mind   gone trouble shooting   amidst galaxies of magnified
crushed flesh   what does it know?   Can't hear the music
Can't feel the fire   Can't see the fairie folk fading into dawn…

Hexed

Night is the Mother of agitation
It's too hot   It's too cold

Blankets oppress you
Blankets neglect you

Night has forgotten her lullaby
Lost her place in your story

Night is the mouth of the cave
Has teeth   Chews up the moon

Night stirs the cauldron
Stews trouble   Drinks dread

> *What if Earth had a bad dream*
> *Shook up the mountain   Shattered the sky*
>
> *What if the buffalo dancers are flung*
> *into the black hole   where once*
>
> *the moon roamed*
> *What if Night is done with us*
>
> *Sucks us back to Chaos*
> > *before first light*
>
> > *What if Night never wakes?*

Wearing Leopard to the Breast Center

Big cats have always stalked your dreams   when did they
spring into fashion   flinging their markings on cottons and
silks   Imbuing your legs and your breasts with their jungle
heat?   They're everywhere   wrapped around the receptionist's
neck   Flaunting their glamour on handbags and iPhones
all over the waiting room   You've got your leopard bra on
for courage   before you hand your tender old girls to the
technician   to be crushed

This is no maidenform fantasy   This is the leap of a predator
her grace   her glory   her claws that rip flesh   This is no
ten thousand dollar fur   requiring a great cat to die for your
glamour   as you stride down some Avenue in Vogue Magazine
This is you wrapped in wild evocation   animal prints on your
bed sheets   your bathrobe   your faux leopard vest

There's a reason those big cats stalk you   track you deep into
dreaming   They smell your nature   Remember the starving
tiger   clawed at your writing hand?   The lion in the library
said he loved you   said he'd eat you?   The sad–eyed leopard
flung herself against your four walls   frantic to break you out?
Oh you've been broken and entered   opened and eaten   ripped
and reborn   Big cat medicine   breathing the dark in some
feline belly   Waking to joy   bruised and weeping

Grandmother Leopard come lie with me   Lick me where
everything aches Rough tongue me back to my rainforest senses
Remember me to the base of my spine   where tail begins its slow
motion Remember my nose   what it knows of earth smells fungi
green growth and scat   Remember the delicate hairs of my ears
the breeze as we leap through the trees   Track me through dances of
shadow and light from sunset to luminous bodies of night   Mark
me as one of your own

Lament of the Replaced   Right Hip

I won't be among the bones   in the cave
of the ancestors   I won't be among the ashes
scattered   on the mountain

I who've been with you since before
first light   who dreamed you
flowering   fingers and toes   flutter kicks

in your mother's no moon dark
When the great waves grabbed you
pushed you down   into dawn   Wasn't I there?

Didn't I stand you up   on wobble feet
gallop you deep   into green woods?
How is it I lost

my grip?   Nothing
connects me to thigh   Bone
strikes bone   I can't bear

your weight   You hobble   you clutch
at walls   tables   door handles
Your dreams slip away   to other beds

The moon   is an empty   begging   bowl

You will take off your rings   your purple
under things   You will lay yourself down
in the no moon dark   You won't know what

hit you   Who was that masked man
who took me as sacrifice?   replaced
by the spawn of some igneous rock?   Titanium

of the old gods   before we were all swallowed
by the new   They say you will dance again
dream again   make love again   but I

who was meant to be   your immortal part
bleached and glowing in the desert sun
must enter the fire
before you

Self Portrait With Ghost

Are we to paint what's on the face, what's inside the face, or what's behind it?

Pablo Picasso

If you should wander in   from Beyond
with your hungry eyes   and your brushes
how would you capture me now?

Your self-portrait   from the bad years
holds my gaze   Look
my face has gathered angles   strong nose

for ghosts   dark brow   well versed
in grief   like yours   A shock
of white mane   I'd have you paint

like the crest of an Alp   were you here to see
how far I've come   from that trembling
girl in a white dress   with red flowers

from half a century ago   Yours was the time
of Picasso   It wasn't your work
to break the world open   to see

what's inside   It wasn't your way
to leap into myth   with minotaur or clown   You painted
the outside   winter trees   family faces

I wonder   how would you capture what glows
in me now?   The burning snake
the dark lady   the lion who tracks

my sun and my rising   the egg I keep
in my pocket   like Jung
to smuggle some god   across borders?

Maybe you'd paint me   writing
Maybe you'd give me   a backdrop
with crescent moons   cups and wands

mysterious Hebrew letters   Maybe
you'd sit me down   by the window
let the tree shine in   as light from behind

a curtain   softens your face from
the bad years   Beyond the seen
is a place   where your hungry eyes

still hold me   and poems begin

I Will Die and Go to My Mother

I will die and go to my Mother   on Devil Mountain
beyond the trees   over the roofs   where rock
touches sky   I will wrap myself up
in my Tree of Life Shawl   and go

Coyote will feast on my tongue   Snake release me
of skin   Magpie assemble my glittering things
The mountain will shake herself   rise
Ask me Her riddles

>   *Who is stopped by nothing?*
>   *Where is the back of beyond?*

I'll be busy shape shifting when I die   Nothing will stop me
from flow   from burning from wind from light on the river
from grass in the meadow   Was I
                                that wild horse girl?

Spirits will greet me

>   *Were we sisters   lovers   neighbors in the region*
>   *of the sun?   Were we bird watchers   star gazers*
>   *subway riders?   What did we do for fun?*

The mountain will lay herself down   will go back to sleep
when I die   Deep below dreaming I'll hear
                                the singing of seeds in the rain

On the Broken Back of Lorca's Story

Time has not washed you away   nor have the rains
in the Puerta del Sol   or sorrow's brown river

They still dream you in Madrid   They feed you
apples and honey   What of

the hungry mouth of your grave   What of
the silver coins that never found your eyes?

Eyes of the Guernica bull   Burning eyes
of my ancestors in the Auto de Fe

Feed me on pomegranate seeds   Long ago
you promised me   what Grandfather Goethe

promised us both   Show me
the face of your death   Hand me

a basket of bone to gather the parts
I need   your gypsy knife   your Harlem feet

your abracadabra tongue   Your blood gets under
my skin   History crushes

your harvest   with purple feet   Time has not
washed you away   nor have the rains

in the Puerta del Sol   nor sorrow's brown river

It's All About Light

It's all about light in Córdoba
river light   leaf light   light of the inner garden
It's all about arches and glimpses of sky
stone flowers   stone curls   stone gathers its vines
into cascades of light
How is it stone turns to shimmer?

It's all about old walls and babies
It's all about high boots and scarves flung just so
                              about the throat

It's all about food in Córdoba
broken eggs with black sausage   aubergines
with honey   bull's tail   fried baby squid
battered anchovies
It's all about olives and wine

It's all about lovers in Córdoba
How is it they shine in the fountains?
How is it that swarms of school children
                     make the cobblestones laugh?

The Guadalquivir reflects the old Roman bridge
makes ovals of its arches

It's all about light in Córdoba
light of the secret Sabbath candles
light from the longing of exile
light from exhumed bones
old light from before the expulsion

before the dimming of Maimonides
before Averroes was banned
before Judah ha Levi left town
                        never to find
                        his Jerusalem

A Song of Granada

There is a flower in Granada
A golden flower with eight petals
A flower of gypsum and alabaster dust
A flower that holds up the sky

I see your face in the fountain
I see your Berber eyes
Clothe me in myrtles and spiraling vines
Let nothing   break the spell

You are my lion of Judah
I am your gate of pomegranate
Your moonflower   your sunflower
Your shimmer   your flow   your longing

Sing me a gated city
Whose ears know the song of the nightingale
Whose eyes know the leap of the faun
Sing me a garden of heaven

Where jasmine and rose intertwine
Where pools reflect forever
Before you become a sack of gold
And I your empty cup

Meet me in the morning
Show me your shrine to the end of our time
An empty shell of alabaster dust
An arabesque of weeping

Where is the son of Granada
Who awakens the sky with his flying horse
Who dresses the mountains in gypsy skirts?
They clap their hands   They sing

There was a flower in Granada
A golden flower with eight petals
A long ago flower that held up the sky
Before the stars were sacked...

About the Author

Naomi Ruth Lowinsky spends morning reverie time working with her dreams, and consulting dream figures, who often leap into her poems. She believes in the power of the unconscious, the magical pull of images, the music of words, the presence of the ancestors and the interpenetration of inner and outer worlds. This collection of poems began when she and her husband travelled to Spain and her poetic ancestor, Lorca began singing to her.

Lowinsky won the Blue Light Poetry Prize for her chapbook, *The Little House on Stilts Remembers*. She also won the Obama Millennial Award and is an International Merit Award Winner in the Atlanta Review 2020 Poetry contest. *Death and His Lorca* is her fifth poetry collection. She is a Jungian Analyst, a member of the San Francisco Jung Institute, and poetry editor for *Psychological Perspectives*. She has led a poetry workshop, *Deep River*, for many years at the San Francisco Jung Institute and recently co-edited an anthology of poems by its participants, *Soul Making in the Valley of the Shadow*. She blogs about poetry and life at sisterfrombelow.com.

Acknowledgements

I am filled with gratitude to the many – living and dead – who have believed in my poetry over the years. Among the beloved dead, are my mother, Gretel Lowinsky, my brother Si Lowinsky, Diane di Prima, Gilda Frantz, Robin Robertson, and Margaret Ryan. Among the beloved living are Patty Cabanas, Carolyn and Phil Cowan, Lucille Lang Day, Sam Kimbles, Mel Matthews, Richard Messer, Cathy Pool, David St. John, Leah Shelleda, Sara Spaulding-Phillips, Alicia Torres, Jan Robinson Vuksinick, the Deep River Poets, and most of all my husband, Dan Safran, who has been my loving companion on all the journeys – inner and outer – that fill this collection.

I am forever grateful to Susan Terris for her masterful help with the manuscript as a whole, to my publisher, Diane Frank, for her enthusiasm and generosity and to Melanie Gendron for her visionary book design, which brought my long–gone grandmother's watercolor to new life and meaning. And of course, eternal thanks to Federico Garcia Lorca, whose *duende* is behind these poems.

Many thanks to the editors of the following publications, in which some of these poems have appeared, often in earlier versions.

Blue Lake Review: "Mother Approaches the Border"
Caliban Online: "Shades of the Gathered and the Gone"
Caveat Lector: "Sometimes   Before First Light"
Circle Show: "Some Questions for the Dream Maker"
Comstock Review: "Tongue"
Diverse Voices Quarterly: "Wearing Leopard to the Breast Center"
Crack the Spine: "Mother's Severed Head"
Darkling: "I Will Die and Go to My Mother"
Dogwood: "Flamenco Dancer"
Empire Review: "When I'm Gone"

Evening Street Press: "Decrescendo of a Musicologist"

Freshwater: "The Angel of Rot"

Jewish Women's Literary Annual: "Your Creation"

Levure Litteraire: "I See You in the Foothills Oma," "Brown on Brown," "Only the Snow Knows," "When Trees Go Wild," "Refuge," "Portrait of the Girl I was Age 14"

Lindenwood Review: "Last Reckoning"

Mantis: "Ghazal In Your Wake"

Monkey Bicycle: "The Shekhinah in Córdoba"

Moon City Press: "Translations from Childhood"

New Millennium Writings: "Your People Are My People," (Won Honorable Mention) "Madelyn Dunham Passing On" (Winner of the Obama Millennium award), "An American History Poem" Paterson Literary Review: "At Nineteen Before She Became My Mother"

Penman Review: "All Night Long I Track the Signs," "Down–Going River Song," "First Infusion"

Prick of the Spindle: "New Hat for the Dreamer"

Psychological Perspectives: "About Our Father," "News from the Dead," "Exodus"

Quiddity: "Elephant Child"

Runes: "A Poem for Persia"

Shark's Reef: "The Russian Woman's Daughter"

Sierra Nevada Review: "Root Canal"

Sliver Stone: "Grandmother Ghost in the Brush Strokes"

Spillway: "Death and His Lorca"

Soundings East: "Lullaby of Lineage"

Stand: "Venus Transit," "I'm Sorry"

Tiger's Eye: "Hexed"

Tightrope: "Past Lives" (Originally published as "Before the Dream Winter"

Visions International: "Córdoba Haunts Me," "It's All About Light," "A Song of Granada"